Healing HURT HEARTS

TRAUMA JOURNAL

This Journal Belongs To:

_____

LATRICE SCOTT, MA, LMHC

BALBOA.PRESS

A DIVISION OF HAY HOUSE

Balboa Press books may be ordered through booksellers or by contacting:

Balboa Press
A Division of Hay House
1663 Liberty Drive
Bloomington, IN 47403
www.balboapress.com
844-682-1282

ISBN: 979-8-7652-3093-0 (sc)
ISBN: 979-8-7652-3094-7 (e)

Print information available on the last page.

Balboa Press rev. date: 08/29/2022

Dedication

"Ouch, That Hurts" is a general response to pain, whether expected or unexpected. However, in my experience, the unexpected pain hurts the most.

I never thought that I would be creating this project by myself, without my best friend, Tangela Sails, with whom this project was birthed.

But here I am on this journey without you. A journey that we planned to complete together.

"Ouch, That Hurts" is the pain I felt when my Mom passed away less than two years later. This hurts the most, but I continue on for you.

Your memory will forever live on.

Contents

"Your vision will become clear only when you can look into your heart. Who looks outside dreams; who looks inside awakes.
~Carl Jung

Introduction- Trauma Defined

Trauma is the Greek word for "Wound".

Trauma has many meanings. It can be defined as a deeply distressing or disturbing experience, emotional shock following a stressful event or a physical injury. Per the American Psychological Association (APA), trauma is an emotional response to a terrible event like an accident, rape or natural disaster. Immediately after the event, shock and denial are typical. Longer term reactions include unpredictable emotions, flashbacks, strained relationships and even physical symptoms like headaches or nausea. While these feelings are normal, some people have difficulty moving on with their lives.

Trauma is the experience of severe psychological distress following any terrible or life-threatening event. Sufferers may develop emotional disturbances such as extreme anxiety, anger, sadness, survivor's guilt, or PTSD. They may experience ongoing problems with sleep or physical pain, encounter turbulence in their personal and professional relationships, and feel a diminished sense of self-worth due to the overwhelming amount of stress.

PTSD, or post-traumatic stress disorder, is an anxiety problem that develops in some people after extremely traumatic events, such as combat, crime, an accident or natural disaster. People with PTSD may relive the event via intrusive memories, flashbacks and nightmares; avoid anything that reminds them of the trauma; and have anxious feelings they didn't have before that are so intense their lives are disrupted.

"Ouch, That Hurts!"

Remember when you were a little child and you scraped your knee? Whether it was from falling off your bike, tripping when running, or being pushed down, it simply hurt, to say the least. When you look at that same knee, can you still see the scar, no matter how faint? Can you still remember how much it hurt? Did you cry? How long did it take for the wound to heal? Were you consoled? After the pain stopped and time passed, did you ride your bike and play again? Did you face your fears?

These physical scars are permanent and still visible today. If you think about what happened in the past long enough, you can continue to relive those moments. The physical pain may be long gone, but many of us continue to suffer emotional, mental, and spiritual pain. Such symptoms include flashbacks, hallucinations, panic attacks, and nightmares; which are often diagnosed as PTSD, Schizophrenia, Bipolar, and a plethora of other mental health disorders. Some of these painful experiences created trauma which manifested into low self-esteem, unforgiveness, mistrust, and paranoia. Now as an adult, you may think you have to handle all of these feelings by yourself. But when you can't manage these feelings alone, depression becomes your enemy and conquers your mind.

This journal's purpose is to help you identify and evaluate your thoughts, feelings, and beliefs regarding trauma you have experienced. Your healing journey is a page away.

How to Use This Journal

This journal is called "Healing Hurt Hearts" because it's important to acknowledge and own your personal trauma(s) in order to effectively address and heal from them.

With any journey, you must first start.

The work that you will be doing will center around your trauma narrative. A trauma narrative is a psychological technique used to help survivors of trauma make sense of their experiences, while also acting as a form of exposure to painful memories. When completing a trauma narrative, the story of a traumatic experience will be told repeatedly through verbal, written, or artistic means.

It is recommended that this trauma journal is completed with a professional counselor. However, this is a self-help journal that can be completed independently. If at any time you feel the need to take a break from this journal, that is okay.

There is no time limit on unpacking your trauma. This is a self-paced journal that can be completed in 6 months, one year, or more.

It's all up to you!

"Trauma leaves 'fingerprints' on the victim. These don't fade when the bruises do."
~Dr. Ellen Taliaferro

The Beginning: My Trauma

"There is no timestampon trauma. There isn't a formula that you can insert yourself into to get from horror to healed. Be patient. Take up space. Let your journey be the balm."
~Dawn Serra

My Trauma:

Who was there:

When did this happen:

Where did this happen:

What happened:

One day my pain will become my cure

My Trauma Symptoms

A Memory I avoid

A flashback I often have

A common nightmare I have

"A whole
Life can be
Shaped by an
old trauma,
remembered
Or not."
Lenore Terr

Pre-Trauma Factors

*Skip any prompts that do not apply

I was diagnosed with the following mental health disorder(s):

As a child, I experienced the following issues:

I was raised to believe:

My parents' relationship affected me in the following ways:

I experienced the following past trauma(s):

My past does not define my future

Ground Myself

After having experienced trauma, it's normal to experience a variety of symptoms such as anxiety, flashbacks, panic attacks, intrusive memories, and other unsettling symptoms.

The following grounding technique will help you to focus on the present.

Five things I can see...

Four things I can feel...

Three things I can hear...

Two things I can smell...

One thing I can taste...

"Owning your story is the bravest thing you will ever do."
Brene Brown

My Trauma (Retelling)

At this time, add more details to your trauma narrative.

Who was there:

When did this happen:

Where did this happen:

What happened:

I will be patient with myself

My Past Trauma

*Skip if this does not apply.

Who was there:

When did this happen:

Where did this happen:

What happened:

"Often the people with the most beautiful hearts are the ones who have endured the greatest pain."
~Karen Salmonsohn

Heart Check

It is important to check in with your heart as you work through your trauma. This brief check in will give you a glimpse of your current feelings and the progress you have made thus far. You can repeat this process as often as you need to.

1) Sit quietly for a few minutes.

2) Identify any areas where you feel tension (i.e. shoulders, neck, back)

3) Pay attention to your breathing (i.e., labored, being held)

4) Identify any tense behaviors (i.e., nail biting, picking at skin, foot tapping)

5) Identify what you are thinking (repetitive thoughts, racing thoughts)

Overcoming
challenges make
my life meaningful

My Thoughts, Feelings, & Beliefs

"It is often in the darkest skies that we see the brightest stars."
~Richard Evans

When I think about what happened...

I Feel:

I Think:

I Believe:

Broken crayons Still color the same

Mindfulness Meditation Exercise

Mindfulness is a type of meditation in which you focus on being intensely aware of what you're sensing and feeling in the moment, without interpretation or judgment.

Mindfulness can be practiced during everyday activities in a variety of ways such as when eating, listening to music, or walking.

1. Find a quiet place. Remove distractions and disconnect from technology.

2. Sit or lie in a comfortable position.

3. Pay attention to your breathing cycle. Notice each breath as it comes in and as it goes out.

4. If your mind wanders, gently notice the wandering and then return to your breathing.

5. If you experience any other distraction, gently notice the distraction and then return to your breathing.

"The soul always knows what to do to heal itself. The challenge is to silence the mind."
~ Caroline Myss

When I think about what happened...

My worst moment was:

I am at peace when I live in the present

Challenging Negative Thoughts

Many people blame themselves for the trauma they have experienced.

Evaluate your current feelings regarding your trauma.

Is there substantial evidence for my thought?

Is there evidence contrary to my thought?

Am I attempting to interpret the situation without all of the evidence?

What would a friend think about this situation?

If I look at the situation positively, how is it different?

Will this matter a year from now?

How about five years from now?

"The **first** step to healing is recognizing that there's a wound."

Recalling My Trauma

I see:

I hear:

I feel:

I taste:

I smell:

MY STRUGGLE WILL NOT BECOME MY IDENTITY

When I think about what happened...

I Feel:

I Think:

I Believe:

"Out of your
vulnerabilities
will come your
strength."
~Sigmund Freud

The Five Senses of Trauma

I saw

I heard

I smelled

I touched/felt

I tasted

My wounds will lead me to my purpose

People/Places that Trigger Traumatic Thoughts

A trigger can be a person, place, or thing that produces an unwanted and/or unexpected emotional response.

My Triggers (Identify at least three):

How I will cope with my triggers:

Resources (Triggers, Pg. 91 & Tips for dealing with triggers, Page 97)

"If you can sit with your pain, listen to your pain, and respect your pain- in time you will move through your pain."
~Bryant McGill

When I think about what happened...

It's okay if your feelings don't change radically, but it's important to continue acknowledging them. "Small" change is still change.

I Feel:

I Think:

I Believe:

What I become
depends on what
I can overcome

Cognitive Distortions (Part 1)

There are 10 common types of cognitive distortions.

Judgment of self and others contributes greatly to cognitive distortions.

It is important to recognize your own cognitive distortions in order to decrease their impact in your life.

Catastrophizing- Expecting the worst outcome in any situation. Example- My boss scheduled a meeting so I'm going to get fired.

Polarized Thinking- Seeing things in black and white extremes. Something is only one way or another.
Example- Today is either good or bad.

Overgeneralization- Applying experiences from one event to another.
Example- My marriage ended in divorce so I should never date again.

Personalization- Blaming yourself for situations that are out of your control; often feeling targeted or attacked.
Example- My daughter is emotionally unavailable because of me.

"Choose your thoughts carefully. Keep what brings you peace, release what brings you suffering. And know that happiness is just a thought away."
~Nishan Panwar

When I think about what happened...

I Feel:

I Think:

I Believe:

My strength will come from overcoming things I didn't think I could

Who Am I Activity (Part 1)

Often times, we believe that who we are is the sum of where we come from, our choices, and our actions.

But WHO YOU ARE is much deeper than that. Discover YOUR TRUE SELF below:

What are my strengths?

What do I love about myself?

What are my weaknesses?

What do I dislike about myself?

"There are wounds
that never show on the
body that are deeper and
more hurtful than anything
that bleeds."

~Laurell K. Hamilton

When I think about what happened...

I Feel:

I Think:

I Believe:

If it costs me my peace, it is too expensive

Automatic Negative Thoughts/ Positive Replacement Thoughts

Automatic Negative Thoughts (ANTS) are thoughts that are often irrational and the result of a situation or trigger.

As discussed earlier, these ANTS are Cognitive Distortions (Refer to Pg. 43, 103)

The good news is that these ANTS can be challenged with Positive Replacement Thoughts (PRTS).

The below activity will help you identify ANTS that follow your triggers. You will also learn how to create positive replacement thoughts.

Trigger	ANT	PRT
No calls/texts	I'm alone.	I have myself.

"The only lasting
trauma is the one
we suffer without
positive change."
~Leo Buscaglia

When I think about what happened...

I Feel:

I Think:

I Believe:

I am making progress each day

Intimacy Activity (Part 1)

Intimacy is more than foreplay and sex. Intimacy is defined as close familiarity or friendship; closeness. Therefore, intimacy can be experienced with a friend, family member, child or romantic partner.

Intimacy is the foundation of forming a strong bond and connection. It requires trust and commitment.

Intimacy can be shared through conversation, quality time, cuddling, hugs, kisses, and sexual activity; to name a few.

Human beings are social creatures that thrive on interaction and touch. When intimacy is missing from our lives, it can lead to feelings of neglect, abandonment, and low self-esteem.

Answer the questions below to assess your current feelings regarding intimacy.

Feel free to skip any question(s) that doesn't apply to you.

When was the last time you experienced intimacy?

How did this experience make you feel?

Have you avoided intimacy in the past?

Are you currently avoiding intimacy?

If yes, why?

When do you feel safe communicating with others?

"Trauma is nothing more than being stuck in what you believe." ~Byron Katie

When I think about what happened...

I Feel:

I Think:

I Believe:

I AM
NOT WHO
THEY SAID
I AM

Intimacy Activity (Part 2)

When we truly trust someone, we place our confidence in them. We depend on them to keep their word. When trust is broken, it can be difficult, even impossible, to restore.

Who do you feel safe communicating with?

Who do you feel comfortable expressing your emotions to?

What higher power do you feel connected to?

If you don't feel connected to a higher power, what are your beliefs? Who do you feel accepted by?

Who understands and accepts the "real" you?

When do you feel free to express yourself sexually? With who?

It's not the load that breaks you down, it's the way you carry it.
~Lena Horne

Heart Check

It is important to check in with your heart as you work through your trauma. This brief check in will give you a glimpse of your current feelings and the progress you have made thus far.

1) Sit quietly for a few minutes.

2) Identify any areas where you feel tension (i.e. shoulders, neck, back)

3) Pay attention to your breathing (i.e., labored, being held)

4) Identify any tense behaviors (i.e., nail biting, picking at skin, foot tapping)

5) Identify what you are thinking (repetitive thoughts, racing thoughts)

The pain I feel today will be the strength I feel tomorrow

The Aftermath: My Healing

"There is no one more deserving of compassion than yourself."

~ Buddha

Healing My Hurt Heart

When we embark on any healing journey, it is important to have a plan to utilize.

This section is focused on your healing, which involves daily introspection. Therefore, I encourage you to journal at least 2 times per week in order to fully benefit from this process.

The following questions act as a guide to help direct you as you heal daily. These questions will be re-evaluated often in this section.

Expect your answers to change as you continue to progress.

What healing do I choose for myself TODAY?

What healing do I choose for myself THIS WEEK?

What healing do I choose for myself THIS MONTH?

What healing do I choose for myself THIS YEAR?

YOUR TRAUMA IS NOT YOUR FAULT, BUT YOUR HEALING IS YOUR RESPONSIBILITY

Who Am I Activity (Part 2)

What do I fear?

What makes me happy?

What are my gifts and talents?

What do I value/cherish most?

What is my life's purpose?

Trauma is a fact of life. It does not, however, have to be a life sentence."
~ Peter A. Levine

Journal Prompt #1

What would I like to change about my life?

I am rediscovering myself and starting over

Healing My Hurt Heart

What healing do I choose for myself TODAY?

What healing do I choose for myself THIS WEEK?

What healing do I choose for myself THIS MONTH?

What healing do I choose for myself THIS YEAR?

"Healing is not an overnight process, it is a daily cleansing of pain, it is a daily healing of your life."
~Leon Brown

Forgiveness Activity

Write a letter to someone you need to forgive.

I will
find the
calm in
the chaos

Journal Prompt #2

How am I a result of the choices I have made?

"Pain will come with time, but time will heal the pain."
~Anthony Liccione

Healing My Hurt Heart

What healing do I choose for myself TODAY?

What healing do I choose for myself THIS WEEK?

What healing do I choose for myself THIS MONTH?

What healing do I choose for myself THIS YEAR?

I am willing to
treat myself
and others
better than the
past ever did

Breathing Activity

Breathing has many benefits. It is believed that when breath is controlled, other aspects of your life can also be influenced.

Our focus is going to be on belly breathing, which has been deemed the best breathing technique.

1) Sit or lie comfortably.

If you're sitting, bend your knees and relax your head, neck, and shoulders. Don't slouch.

If you're lying down, place a small pillow under your head and one under your knees to enhance your comfort. As an alternative, you can keep your knees bent.

2) Place one hand on your upper chest and place the other hand right above your navel.

3) Breathe in slowly through your nose so that you feel your stomach rise with your other hand. The hand on your chest should remain still.

4) Breathe out through your mouth and let your belly relax. You'll feel the hand above your navel fall inward as the hand on your chest continues to remain still.

Healing comes
when
we choose to walk
away from darkness
and move towards
a brighter light.

~Dieter F. Uchtdor

Journal Prompt #3

What are some limiting beliefs I have about myself ? How can I change them?

I forgive because I deserve peace

Healing My Hurt Heart

What healing do I choose for myself TODAY?

What healing do I choose for myself THIS WEEK?

What healing do I choose for myself THIS MONTH?

What healing do I choose for myself THIS YEAR?

"Trauma creates
change you
don't choose.
Healing creates
change you
do choose."
~Michele Rosenthal

Safe Space Activity

Creating an internal and/or external safe space is necessary for your peace of mind.

It's a fact of life that your thoughts, feelings, beliefs, and situations will sometimes be chaotic.

These are the times when having a safe space will come in handy. First, think about the last time you felt safe.

Where are you? Is anyone there with you or are you alone?

What time of day is it (morning, afternoon, evening)?

What do you see?

What do you hear?

What do you feel? Are you sitting, standing, or lying down?

If you are eating, what do you taste? Salty? Sweet? Sour?

I RECEIVE HEALING ENERGY

Journal Prompt #4

How do I embrace my imperfections?

"I'm still coping with my trauma, but coping by trying to find different ways to heal it rather than hide it."
~Clementine Wamariya

Healing My Hurt Heart

What healing do I choose for myself TODAY?

What healing do I choose for myself THIS WEEK?

What healing do I choose for myself THIS MONTH?

What healing do I choose for myself THIS YEAR?

Healing
cannot occur
in the
absence of
self-love and
compassion

Triggers

Even if you aren't familiar with how to handle a gun, you may understand that once the trigger is pulled, a cycle of pain has been initiated. Being triggered mentally and emotionally is very similar to an individual that is being held at gunpoint.

They're often unsure of what will happen next and are hoping for the best outcome.

Their best bet would have been to be prepared for a situation in which they would have to face a trigger.

The same philosophy can be utilized when thinking of mental triggers. Triggers are external events or circumstances that may produce very uncomfortable emotional or psychiatric symptoms such as anxiety, panic, discouragement, despair, or negative self-talk.

Common triggers include feeling overwhelmed, the end of a relationship, physical illness, loud noises, being yelled at, being judged, being around someone that treated you badly, financial problems, and spending too much time alone.

The most common ways to deal with triggers are to avoid them, reduce your exposure to them, or face them head on. When facing triggers head on, you will need a strategy which can include coping skills, a support system you can contact, and pre-planned responses.

"There is no true healing unless there is a change in outlook, peace of mind and inner happiness."
~Edward Bach

Journal Prompt #5

Write a love letter to yourself.

This current moment is all that matters

Healing My Hurt Heart

What healing do I choose for myself TODAY?

What healing do I choose for myself THIS WEEK?

What healing do I choose for myself THIS MONTH?

What healing do I choose for myself THIS YEAR?

"My past has not defined me, destroyed me, deterred me, or defeated me; it has only strengthened me."
~Steve Maraboli

Triggers Activity

Triggers often come in the form of a person, place or situation. Triggers often provoke unwanted emotions and behaviors. In order to effectively deal with your triggers, they must be identified. Then strategies can be created for avoidance, reduction of exposure, and coping.

Identify and describe your three common triggers:

Discuss your strategy for avoiding or reducing exposure to these triggers:

Discuss your strategy for facing these triggers when they can't be avoided:

I am
responsible
for my healing

Journal Prompt #6

How can I make peace with the things I cannot change?

"We repeat what we don't repair."
~Christine Langley-Obaugh

Healing My Hurt Heart

What healing do I choose for myself TODAY?

What healing do I choose for myself THIS WEEK?

What healing do I choose for myself THIS MONTH?

What healing do I choose for myself THIS YEAR?

No matter what I've been through, My story is not over

Cognitive Distortions (Part 2)

Mind Reading- Making negative assumptions about a person's intentions or thoughts.
Example- My significant other didn't answer the phone so they must be avoiding me.

Mental Filtering- Viewing yourself and your life negatively, while ignoring the positive.
Example- My event wasn't a success because the room wasn't full.

Discounting the Positive- Not acknowledging when something good happens.
Example- It was a coincidence that I passed the test.

"Should" Statements- Often placing blame on yourself or others for what "should" have happened.
Example- I should be less fearful of flying.

Emotional Reasoning- Relying on emotions and/or feelings versus facts.
Example- I feel fat even though my BMI is healthy.

Labeling/Mislabeling- Assigning negative labels to yourself and others based on one past behavior or situation.
Example- I'm a bad driver because I was involved in a car accident.

Healing takes courage, and we all have courage, even if we have to dig a little to find it
~Tori Ames

Journal Prompt #7

What can I do today that my future self will thank me for?

I can't change the world, but I can change my world

Healing My Hurt Heart

What healing do I choose for myself TODAY?

What healing do I choose for myself THIS WEEK?

What healing do I choose for myself THIS MONTH?

What healing do I choose for myself THIS YEAR?

"Turn Your Wounds Into Wisdom."
~Oprah Winfrey

Cognitive Distortions Activity

In order to challenge your cognitive distortions (ANTS), you must identify your triggers and become aware of your thoughts and emotions. Your thoughts and emotions precede your behaviors. Lastly, it's important to create Positive Replacement Thoughts (PRTS).

Self-Evaluate at least once weekly.

Situations	Thoughts	Emotions	Behaviors	PRTS

A healed heart is the ultimate treasure.

Journal Prompt #8

What do I need to Start, Stop, & Continue in my life?

"Healing and wholeness are for those willing to be vulnerable enough to be made strong."

~Julie Yarbrough

Heart Check

It is important to check in with your heart as you work through your trauma. This brief check in will give you a glimpse of your current feelings and the progress you have made thus far.

1) Sit quietly for a few minutes.

2) Identify any areas where you feel tension (i.e. shoulders, neck, back)

3) Pay attention to your breathing (i.e., labored, being held)

4) Identify any tense behaviors (i.e., nail biting, picking at skin, foot tapping)

5) Identify what you are thinking (repetitive thoughts, racing thoughts)

*(P. 79, Breathing Activity)

"When we deny our stories, they define us. When we own our stories, we get to write a brave new ending."

~Brene Brown

Personal Stories

TRAUMA HAS A SOUND
By: Dorothy Pierre-Joseph

If I could sum up the totality of my life's trauma, I would have to say it is a sound that echoes so loudly that had you asked me a few years ago, I would say it was audible.

It started with three knocks at the door. This was not unusual. As a matter of fact, nothing was absent from the norm that day. I didn't get any eerie feelings. It was a typical Saturday in our home. My chores were done and I was babysitting my younger brother. I listened to the music mom would not allow me to listen to. I knew to turn it off by nine, which was close to the time I knew mom would be home. It was no different than any other night. As we had done so many times before as we heard a knock at the door, 'boom, boom, boom!" I opened the door for my mom since she had groceries in her hand and needed an extra hand. Immediately as I opened the door, she came flying in with two armed men following and pressing close behind her. The three of us were in shock, but had no time to try to reason with what was happening. I can recall all of our jewelry and money being taken. Had that been all they took, we would have been fine. It would not have changed the trajectory of all of our lives the way that it did. My mother was raped that night in her bedroom. My brother and I were witnesses as we heard her desperate cries and intense sobbing from her room. We were hopeless and helpless. Fast forward twenty plus years later in the future and you will find those three characters still scrambling to pick up the pieces. Trauma is so caustic. It intensifies and spreads rampantly if left untreated. I became a psychiatric nurse and my job was literally helping those who were broken and seemingly irreparable; those that suffered from mental disease from early childhood or adult onset.

I came up with treatment plans with a team of other mental health professionals to ensure favorable outcomes to enable many to have quality of life. I worked psychiatric units that included recurring patients attempting suicide and others in a state of mania. Most common were those that had become so despondent and so hopeless they became victims to their own minds. I seemed to thrive at work. I felt quite accomplished, but somehow empty. The sound would echo in and out. I stayed busy to not deal with the sound. I got married to a wonderful man and had five beautiful children. I tried to hide the sound in the folds of my spouses love and the responsibilities of parenthood.

It was in fact during my last pregnancy where everything I knew collapsed. It was a very difficult pregnancy. After about the third time of going into premature labor, I was advised to go on bed rest. For the first time, I had to stop working and leave the kids to my husband. Now, I had a lot of time alone, and to myself, and to my thoughts. The days were all consumed with the sound "boom, boom, boom", crying and sobbing, and the many other sounds I had been repressing from childhood; like the creaking floor boards that would scream as my assailant would get closer during my early years of sexual assault as a child; the slamming doors as I would see my father take my mom by force into the room with all brute force and overtake her with his lack of control; the sound of the other inmates as they conversed with family through thick, bullet proof glass in the prison where my little brother was held. Yes, that same little brother never really picked up those broken pieces either. The sounds vibrated on and on and I was trapped. They amplified until it was silent.

When I could accept what was happening, I realized I had an episode of my own. I was in a psychiatric unit at a local hospital after attempting suicide while almost six months pregnant. I was scared, and once again, I was that teenager from over twenty years ago trying to deal with the sound. I could no longer hide behind my career, spouse, or children. I sat in group sessions next to patients I had treated and next to colleagues I worked with for many years. I had to confront the trauma. The journey was long and demanding, but I had the opportunity to free myself and heal.

What is my final assessment, not only as a professional, but as a survivor? The first would be to seek help and treatment as soon as possible. Counseling should be initiated after any assault, whether you are the victim, or a witness of the assault. Secondly, identify a support system and learn to question things that seemingly evoke an unpleasant reaction which could possibly be a trigger for you. Lastly, I would say don't be afraid of the sound. On the other side is the sound of freedom and that is beautiful. You deserve to be the narrator of your story.

ANONYMOUS

Emotional and physical abuse was very prominent in my adolescent years. My mom's nurturing ceased the day she heard me call her a bitch at 13 years old. I only said it because I was showing off in front of my friends, but little did I know at the time, that sealed the deal. FOREVER! She stopped providing for me altogether. One night, with no reason, she came into my room and said, "I bet you're fucking bigger dicks than me." I was a virgin at the time. That statement led me to losing my virginity because I didn't want to prove her wrong. She used to beat me with tennis rackets, frying pans, and anything else she was able to get her hands on. She was infamous for her sneak attacks. This is when she would coax me into putting my guard down, then WHAM!!, a slap or punch to the face would knock me to the ground. I eventually moved in with my grandmother, but that didn't lead to any halt in the abuse.

My grandmother was a private duty nurse that worked away from home 3 to 4 nights out of the week. I was left in the care of my baby uncle and he was very abusive. I remember one day he had company over and wanted me to leave the house. I had gotten suspended from school for fighting so I really had nowhere to go. I went into my grandmother's room to give him privacy, but that wasn't enough. He proceeded to come into the room and drag me out by my hair, breaking my nails. I was in utter shock when his company sat there and didn't say anything. I was thrown out of the house with nowhere to go but roam the apartment complex like a lost child. A lost soul. He would pounce on me for things like messing with his cassette tape collection or saying something that rubbed him the wrong way. Adding insult to injury, around this time is when inappropriate touching began between myself and my 2nd generation cousins. I never looked at it as molestation because it was consensual.

But now that I'm an adult, I'm very clear as to exactly how inappropriate it was. All of these occurrences were deeply suppressed, yet the pain and brokenness showed up in major ways during my adult life. I've been in several domestically violent relationships; even landing myself in jail twice. I was once facing 20 years in prison for an aggravated assault charge, but I'm grateful it was reduced to disorderly conduct. To be quite honest, violence seemed to be a normal way of showing love to my partners because it's all I knew. I was able to attract a mate that loved everything about me. From my alien shaped forehead to my moodiness. He got it the worst because he refused to give up on me. I did everything possible to break him, unintentionally. I broke him physically and emotionally, but his love never wavered until about the 8th year of our relationship.

Eventually loyalty has its breaking point when treated unjust. He then began to return the violence and that's when the tables turned. No one deserved the treatment I was dishing out. It wasn't until I became tired of myself when I realized that I was unhealthy for everyone around me; even my children. I wasn't nearly as bad toward my children as my mom was towards me, but when my buttons were pushed too many times, I literally exploded to a place of no return. I always knew I didn't want to be like my mom, yet I was like her in many ways. It took my uncle passing away for me to confront my demons by confronting her and unleashing all of my hurt, pain and anger. It was a well overdue release that eventually launched me into healing my wounds that were covered with bandages all these years. Though I have a long way to go, I've come so far. It takes a great deal of maturity to look at yourself in the mirror while calling yourself out on your bullshit.

How I treat others is how I will be treated. Life is one big reflective mirror that works like a boomerang. You get what you give, so with that, I'm learning to heal myself by giving the best of myself to others without seeking anything in return. Peace and Love!

A Crossroads Experience
By: Frederick Beaty

We have all entered into a crossroads experience. We have all come to a point in our lives where we stand in the middle of the road with the obvious paths before us, with a choice to make, and the consequences of that choice. Everyone's crossroads experience is different and we all have experienced something traumatic that may have led us down this painful road. Bear with me, because this ride may get a little bumpy. This is my crossroads experience.

I put my son to rest on July 13th 2015, nine days after he was shot and killed by a Newport News Police detective. The initial shock and awe quickly turned into pain, that pain quickly turned into grief, that grief slowly turned into anger, and that anger turned into despair. Two months later, my father-in-law passed, and I set aside my grief to help my wife and her family through their process, while still trying to make sense of (and try to understand) my own process. I still had no idea where I was in my process and I was desperately trying to find out. Well, I found out that I was in the anger stage of my grieving, as I had lost two very good jobs and had lost at least a couple more due to my anger and my increasingly absent sense of responsibility. My marriage was hanging on by a very thin thread and I had begun to drink heavily. I buried myself in my emotions. I questioned every part of my manhood, brooded over the fact that I failed my son in every possible way, not to mention I failed my other children as well. I held so much inside, but no one knew it.

My crossroads experience came when we had to move from our home and were forced to live with one of my wife's friends. This was at a time when our grandchildren were living with us and I felt that it was my fault that we were in this situation.

We got into another argument and she had really laid into me, which in turn really hurt. I went back to put on some clothes and spoke to a couple of temp agencies to see what was available. After that, I parked in a parking lot and pulled out the knife that I had grabbed from the kitchen. I had tried to kill myself four times and four times it did not work. I had even failed at ending my own life. The tears just flowed like a broken dam.

I cried so hard that I had an asthma attack and threw up. I looked at myself and knew I was at my crossroads. I had a difficult choice to make, one that would change my life's trajectory. I did not want to continue feeling the way I did and I wanted peace in my life.

A choice to make with two paths before me. Well, I chose to walk straight; a medium of the two paths, if you will. Through prayer, counseling, and understanding some very hard truths about myself, I found a safe haven for my emotions and I started to gain the peace I had so desperately wanted.

My confidence began to be renewed and I made concerted strides to believe in myself again. But the one thing I gained was the understanding of my mission; to share my experience and be transparent so those that enter that experience emerge from it enabled, powerful, and victorious. Paths forward are always the result of a crossroads experience and we have all come to that point in our lives where we have stared down a fork in the road. Many people look at this as an opportunity to either go left or right, thinking that one path is the "right" path and one path is the "wrong" path, when in actuality, there is no right or wrong path.

The path you choose is the path you choose and there is no timetable on your arrival to wherever your destination is. The one thing that I had to understand is that no one travels alone and that Yahweh is ever present in our travels, either in front of us, beside us, behind us or carrying us.

LONG LIVE ERIC BLOCKER
By: Tahira Walker

I am a victim of gun violence and this is my testimony. On August 9, 2017, my friend Eric and I were sitting in my car after a get together waiting for a friend to come when someone walked up to my car and began shooting. My friend was shot multiple times and brutally killed right before my eyes. I was shot once in my lower back and grazed once on my right butt cheek.

I had to wear a colostomy bag for 9 months. My stomach was cut 19 inches long, 3 inches wide and 3 inches deep to save my life. I was basically looking at the inside of my stomach. With that being said, the bullet I was shot with was stuck in my side for the whole 9 months. When I received my reverse colostomy surgery in May 2018, the bullet was surgically removed. The individuals responsible for this took away my friend, my happiness, my joy, my urge to keep going, my self-esteem, and my peace of mind.

They destroyed families and hurt loved ones. There were times I wanted to give up on everything. There was a possibility that I was going to get discharged from the military because of my condition. I felt like my whole world was crashing. Every day I would look at myself in the mirror and just cry because I wasn't happy with the way I looked.

Looking at a bag connected to me for 9 months really hurt me, knowing my body would NEVER look the same. I lost A LOT of weight. There were times I couldn't even recognize who I was because of how different I looked. I lost interest in doing things because I was worried about what people would say about me being skinny. I even had people who thought it was funny that I had to wear a colostomy bag. When I accepted everything that happened, I knew God had a plan for me and that he wasn't finished with me. I am a walking miracle. After numerous people told me I had a purpose because He gave me a second chance, I had no choice but to believe it.

God gave me a second chance to tell my story and make a change somehow. Special thanks to my support system that's been here for me since day one. They kept me motivated, positive, and made sure I NEVER gave up.

I outgrew a lot of people and met a lot of amazing people during my journey that haven't left my side. I wanted to tell the story about my battle wounds. They symbolize strength and courage. BY THE GRACE OF GOD, I AM HEALED AND STRONGER THAN EVER. I WAS ALSO MEDICALLY CLEARED TO FULLY GO BACK INTO THE MILITARY AND I'M ABLE TO PICK UP WHERE I LEFT OFF. God Is Good. I'm back and BETTER. If He did it for me, He definitely can do it for you.

#LONGLIVEERICBLOCKER

Our story will FOREVER be heard as long as I live.

A BOY NAMED "DUSTY"
By: Harlo Hendrix

My first encounter with racism and bullying came at the hands of a red headed boy named "Dusty." I was in the eighth grade and had just returned from living with my grandmother in the deep South, where I had attended an all-black school. Needless to say, this traumatic tale recounts my experience and the profound effect it had on me.

First day of 8th Grade:

Days prior, I had been mentally preparing for the first day of school. It would be my last year as a junior high student, so I hoped to acquire some friendships that would flourish into high school. I opted not to wear any of the designer clothing my father and grandmother sent as a "back to school" gift. One thing I learned from always being the new kid at school is that the attire you selected for the first day of school would definitely determine the tone of the rest of the year. I opted to wear a pair of gray sweats and a matching hoodie; comfortable enough to fit into the general school population and obscure enough for me to hide in the shadows of my social discomfort. However, as I entered the halls of my new school, I would quickly learn that there was no hoodie, cloak or cover that would help me blend into the shadows.

I stood out like a brown unicorn in a stable full of ALL white horses which was a perfect contradiction from the school I had attended the year before. There I was just one of the herd. There I occasionally stood out because my academic performance was more advanced. As I walked down the hall to the attendance office where I had been instructed to pick up my class schedule, I could feel the piercing stares and glares that questioned my presence. I knew in that moment that no outfit or level of intelligence would ever allow me to fit in.

On the bus ride home to the dilapidated apartments I lived in, tucked behind the local state university amongst the towering trees, literally and figuratively across the railroad tracks, I was forced to sit next to a red headed juvenile delinquent named Dusty. Dusty immediately squealed, "I don't want this black nigger sitting next to me." As the bus full of white students erupted into laughter, I felt a queasiness in the pit of my stomach. This felt different than other school experiences I had thus far. The overwhelming desire to defend myself was stifled by the reality that I was outnumbered. My response would have only erupted into a physical altercation to which I was destined to lose. As I looked for someone, anyone to come to my defense, I briefly locked eyes with the bus driver, who only offered a look of empathy.

For the next several weeks, I endured racial slurs, intrusive comments, and snickers from the kids in the hall. During that time, I learned that I was not the only brown unicorn in the stable. There was a total of four of us; one male and two other females. The male unicorn seemed adjusted to his surroundings. The other students treated him with a noticeable range of acceptance while one of the other female unicorns masked herself to appear as if she were one of them. Her deep tan and hair texture were not characteristics that could be easily overlooked. However, they all seemed to play along with her. As for myself and the other female unicorn, we simply hid our horns and held our heads low. We even avoided one another just to discourage any unwarranted attention.

I would suffer silently through the classes, but it was the bus ride home that I feared the most. Riding through all of the high-end homes, fantasizing what it would be like to ever live in one, my thoughts would be routinely interrupted by the bellowing of Dusty calling me "BLACK NIGGER BITCH!"

By this time, most of the students had become bored with his antics and only a few would engage, which only motivated him to be more brutal with his insults. It was the day that Dusty decided that my life was of no value that I was truly changed.

I told my mother and her response was to beat his ass if he touched me and she'd deal with the consequences later. Her advice was neither practical or helpful. I tried to confide in the school counselor as suggested by the Principal who concluded that Dusty's actions were a clear indication of his attraction towards me.

"Dusty is a good kid. He would never hurt you. If anything, he probably likes you," she said. "I'll talk to Dusty. I'm sure you will be friends before you know it."

I had exhausted all of the channels that I thought could help me. One of the worst feelings I've ever had was having my pleas for help dismissed as some ploy for attention.

Presumably after the counselor addressed my issue with Dusty, he too realized that anything I said about him was inconsequential. He proved that on our last bus ride together.

On this particular day after school, the bus driver stopped me as I got on the bus. He was an older white gentleman in his mid-to-late 50's. He reminded me of Mr. Roper from the show "Three's Company". Until that point, he had never uttered a word to me. I had only caught his subtle glances through his rearview mirror on the daily ride home.

He said to me, "One of the highlights of my day since school started was being greeted with your pretty little smile. You haven't smiled for me lately and I just wanted to make sure you were okay."

I politely shrugged my shoulders and took the first empty seat I could find next to the window so that I wouldn't be shoved to the floor as I had been in the past. As I sat down, I found a little comfort in the bus driver's words. Someone had noticed me. Someone had seen my unicorn horn and recognized it's beauty.

Just as I began to indulge in my first sense of feeling mildly comfortable, Dusty plopped down into the empty space next to me. He moved in closer towards me. This was the closest he or any of the other students had ever been to me intentionally. I could feel his breath next to my ear, causing me to feel nauseous by his closeness. He was in violation of my personal space and I was paralyzed with fear. Suddenly the pressure of his fist against the side of my leg forced me to notice the silver switchblade he was holding in his hand.

"You tried to get me in trouble nigger? When you get off the bus, I'm gonna cut your throat and throw you in the creek," he snarled into my ear. We sat silently next to each other. When he didn't exit the bus at his normal stop, which was five stops before mine, I began to worry. I began plotting my escape. I had even thought about getting off at a different stop with other students, but I couldn't count on any of them to help me.

I was always last to get off the bus. Dusty stayed on the bus until we were the only two students left. By this time, he'd moved to the empty seat in front of me. He then began to whisper menacingly towards me, "I'm gonna kill you, blacky, like the stinking dog you are. I'm gonna slit your fucking throat as soon as we get off this bus." My heart began racing. I could feel the vessels near my temple begin to throb as sweat and tears streamed down my face. I managed to meekly yell, "LEAVE ME ALONE!" Although it felt as if I had used every muscle in my body to yell those words, I didn't think the bus driver heard me. But just as I opened my eyes to face my demon, the bus came to a sudden stop.

The mild-mannered bus driver jumped up as Dusty scurried to the empty seat across from me, trying to appear innocent of any wrong doing.

"Dusty!", he yelled sternly, "What are you still doing on my bus?"

"Going to a friend's," Dusty replied.

"Not today," he remarked as he grabbed Dusty by his jacket collar and physically removed him from the bus.

As Dusty resisted his removal, he hurled threats at the bus driver.

"You can't touch me. I'm gonna get you fired!"

But his last threat was directed towards me.

"I'm still gonna kill you fucking nigger."

When the bus driver returned, I could see the apologetic sadness in his eyes. He sat next to me on the now empty bus and asked, "How long has this been going on, dear?"

"Since the first day of school, sir," I confessed, staring down at the floor feeling inexplicably shameful and remorseful.

"Why didn't you tell someone?" he questioned.

"I did."

He leaned back in the seat, letting out a sigh of exasperation, and then abruptly returned to the driver's seat. He dropped me off at the final stop.

Dusty never rode the bus to school in the mornings, so that was usually the time I took to mentally prepare for a day of shun and ridicule. As I exited, the bus driver stopped and asked that I accompany him to the Principal's office.

"You're not in trouble", he assured me.

As we entered the main office, "Mr. Bus Driver" (I never knew his name) requested to speak with the Principal and was immediately shown to the office. I was asked to remain in the waiting area.

After what seemed like several long minutes, the door opened and I was invited in. The Principal proceeded to ask a lot of questions and offered what I presumed to be a sincere apology for my experience. I was excused and allowed to return to class.

I never saw Dusty again. I also never saw "Mr. Bus Driver" again. I heard whispers from other students that Dusty had been expelled for the incident on the bus. Other rumors insinuated that the bus driver's threats caused Dusty to fear attending school. I'd imagined those who believed the latter would have also been the ones that would have helped him assault me.

I never had a chance to thank "Mr. Bus Driver", but I have found ways to honor him. He championed for me. He stood up for me.

We live in a world today that is plagued by high numbers of suicidal teens and adolescents. I recognize the signs because there were moments during my Dusty experience that I contemplated suicide. To not be heard during daily threats of violence against you and to be dismissed and have your pleas for help ignored or shelved is a low and diminishing feeling. If this man had not recognized the severity of what I was experiencing, if it had not been for his simple act of humanity; I can't be sure if Dusty would have carried out his threats or if I would have succumbed to my attempts. I never worried about seeing Dusty again because my mother and I routinely moved.

As a nomadic latchkey kid, I never stayed at a school for more than two semesters. As for those friendships I hoped to attain, I never even met another student there. Although my "would be" assailant was out of sight, he would never be out of mind completely. His is a name I would never forget.

I remember him when I read stories about Felicia, Rose, Darren and a countless number of others who took their own lives feeling muted by social, sexual and racial stigmas. I remember him when I read or hear about the senseless deaths of Tamika, Michelle and others murdered by the hatred of those social, sexual and racial stigmas.

Bullying, racism, and hate crimes are often the same in nature and accompany one another. It is often a learned behavior trickled down from generations of social dysfunction and ignorance.

I honor "Mr. Bus Driver" by being observant and compassionate towards my own children's behavior and of those that I come in contact with. I recognize their smile or lack their-of.

I listen to the subtle remarks that express discontent. I talk and I listen because I recognize that in that moment, I could be saving a life; either at the hands of another or their own.

Daddy's Little Nightmare
By: Tarena Tutt

I never quite understood why my Daddy chose not to be in my life. The irony of it all is that we look just alike. As a little girl, I would get a call from him promising to come and pick me up on Saturday. I would get so excited, pack up my best clothes, and my favorite bear, Lucky. I woke up early on Saturday morning like a kid on Christmas day.

My stomach rumbled with nerves of excitement and anticipation. I rushed to finish my morning routine. I looked at my Mom with excitement in my brown eyes. She knew the look so she would say go ahead and call him and see what time he's coming. I picked up the phone and used my little fingers to make the numbers go in a circle. I nervously listened to the rings as I waited for him to answer the phone.

I paced back and forth as the phone rang. One ring, two rings, three rings, four rings, and five rings. This is when my tears would begin to build up.

He answered the phone and I took a deep breath, then asked, "Daddy, what time are you coming?", with the sweetest voice.

My daddy answered, "I'll be there at 9. Let me go and get ready."

I hung up the phone with the biggest smile on my face. I grabbed Lucky and my bag and stood in the window, not wanting to miss a second of his arrival. My mom told me she would call me when he came, but I told her I wanted to keep waiting by the window. I watched every car and truck drive by.

The neighbors walked by and we would wave at each other. I noticed that the time had passed for my daddy to arrive. Another hour passed with me standing in the window and I could hear my mom calling my daddy asking him if he was still coming. My ears perked up as I eavesdropped. My mom stood next to me and told me he was running late but would pick me up in an hour.

My mom offered me a snack, but I refused. I just wanted to keep waiting for my daddy. My mom looked in my eyes and gave me a hug. She encouraged me to sit on the couch with her and said she would wait with me. But I wanted to keep standing at the window so I wouldn't miss my daddy when he pulled up. Another hour passed, but this time when my mom called him, there was no answer. I became over excited because I thought that meant he was really on his way. I screamed when I saw a white truck turn the corner thinking it was my daddy, but it drove by.

My mom couldn't stand to see me suffer any longer and told me he wasn't coming. She gave me a big hug and told me it was time for dinner. I turned to her with tears in my eyes and asked her why he didn't come. My mom told me she didn't know as I cried in her arms. She carried me to the couch and patiently rocked me until I cried myself to sleep.

The next morning, I found myself with a face full of tears and a growling stomach. My mom walked in my room and wiped my tears. She kissed me on my forehead and told me she made my favorite breakfast. As a 7-year-old child, I couldn't grasp why he had lied to me. I wondered what I did to make my dad hate me.

Why Are You So Angry?

By: Janeice Smith-Alexandre

Are you easily frustrated by everything and anything? Do you go from "zero to one hundred real quick?" If so, you aren't alone. There are millions of people across the world that deal with anger issues daily. Anger is a huge aspect of how a survivor copes with life's stressors and traumas. Take Tina and Sean for example. These two teenagers come from families and homes that do not provide consistency, safety or comfort. We're talking about being abused by caregivers, being bullied by siblings, and over all being emotionally and physically neglected. In order to avoid their pain, they use anger as a survival tool to shift their focus and block their true feelings.

Although many anger issues are linked to experiencing some type of trauma, this is not the reason for all cases. We are all the walking wounded and have experienced some type of injustice. How we respond to these injustices varies depending on many factors.

However, one common response to injustice or an unfair event in which we have been belittled or made a victim is anger. Let's use Timothy and Stacy as an example. Timothy and Stacy have been married for over 10 years. Timothy has always been the sole provider for his family, until recently. Timothy's job cut back on his working hours with no explanation as to why. The cut interfered with providing for Stacy and the kids. Timothy felt like less of a man and began to turn to alcohol as a solution. He often came home inebriated which led him to fight with his wife almost daily.

In this case, Timothy feels angry because he feels betrayed by his employer of 15 years and Stacy has anger in her heart because she feels betrayed by the person who vowed to protect her.

As you can infer by our examples, there is undoubtedly a relationship between trauma and anger. As a School Counselor, several scholars are referred to me because of the anger they display at school. Once I establish a rapport with these students, they begin to open up and we're able to identify the cause of their anger. Some of these students use anger as a coping skill because they're in group homes, neglected by parents, can't read, witnessed a parent being murdered and so much more.

I always tell my scholars that it's okay to be angry as it is a normal healthy emotion. Anger itself isn't the problem. However, anger can cause us to make unhealthy choices. When we are angry, there are many changes we experience in our bodies. Physically, our faces may become red, our blood pressure rises, our tone of voice becomes louder, among a number of other cues.

How can we learn to recognize and deal with anger before things turn violent? The answer is easy. It is important to utilize anger management skills. I work with my scholars on building their list of techniques. Their list is taped to their desk so that they have a visual resource to refer to. Some of the coping skills my scholars use are ripping up paper, going to a calming corner (which their teacher has assisted me in identifying in the classroom), inhaling and exhaling, putting the palms of their hands together, push and release, using a stress ball and drawing pictures.

Overall, anger can be caused by many things. However, we can control the way we respond to anger before things turn violent.

ANONYMOUS

We all know that there is an appointed time for one to leave this earth. The question is When? Where? We all try to do our best to prepare, but the reality is that you can never be prepared for this event in life. I never really knew how hard the death of a loved one can hit you until I experienced it. I mean, I had lost my great grandmother, cousin, and a neighbor, but I really didn't feel it the most until I lost my parents. Yes, that's right. I said parents. Anyone who knows me knows that I loved my parents. I was what you would call a Daddy's girl and a Mama's girl. I could count on them and when they got older and their health began to deteriorate, they could count on me to be there to take care of them.

My parents were there from Pre-K to when I graduated college and beyond. They were even present at my special milestone in adulthood—Marriage. Wait, let's go back. My parents were quite healthy from what I can remember. It was when I went off to college in 2000 when their health started to take a turn for the worse. It started when my mom was diagnosed with Diabetes in 2001. She was a school cafeteria worker, but decided to retire when her health would not allow her to continue to work. She began her day by giving herself insulin shots. She did this twice a day. She started to get better. At least I thought she was.

As the years passed, I finished college and came back home to establish a life of my own. I had moved out and everything. I remember getting calls in the middle of the night about my father. He was in and out of the hospital. I could never get the full story from my mother and siblings, but his condition was a lot worse than what I was told. I literally watched my father go from an outgoing man who loved his family and loved to drive to a man confined to a wheelchair.

I began to get angry. I was angry with my mom and my siblings because I felt that they were holding back the real information as to what was going on with my father. I took days off from work and stayed with him to make sure he took his medication. God even allowed him to make it to my wedding in 2014. He was in a wheelchair, but he was there. I will never forget the day he passed. He had been in the hospital for about two weeks. I made it my business to go see him everyday, despite what everyone said about me going. They were worried because I was 8 months pregnant with my first child and his first grandchild. It was during Christmas time and we were going into 2015. On the morning of New Year's Eve, I had a dream that my dad and I were in a grocery store. It was weird because he was walking around like he used to.

I was just about to touch him when my husband woke me up. I immediately headed to see my mom. When I arrived, everybody was asking me where I had been. I told them I was at home. Apparently, they tried to reach me to tell me that my dad had passed. On my way there, I heard a song on the radio,

"I hope you dance", that reminded me of my dad and I began to cry. But this cry was different. It was like peace came over me. God had already prepared me for what I was going to hear. So there I was at my mom's house crying. I was thinking "How?" and I didn't know what to do. My dad was my best friend, my movie watching partner, my heart, and he was gone. I was told by everyone to take it easy because I was carrying my son. I did. I began to hold everything in to the point that I had to have an emergency C-section 7 days later.

Yes, 7 days later my son was here. I was thinking if he could have held on a little longer, he would have seen his very first grandchild. I began to get angry, depressed, anxious, and worried. I even started isolating myself. I went through postpartum, although I didn't understand it at the time. On top of that, me and my partner began to have issues. All I could think of every time something would go wrong is that if my dad was here this would not be happening. He would bail me out. He would help me. He would tell me what to do. This went on for years. Even up to my mother's passing.

My mother passed in 2018, 4 months after her mother passed, of the same thing my father passed from. My mother was 72 years old. She was a strong woman who tried her best to fight through what she had. She got a chance to see all three of her grandchildren. What is so significant about her death is that she passed on the very day I was due to have my daughter which was 10/9/2018. I ended up having my daughter early in September due to health reasons.

The Blind Eye
By: Natasha Jean

I'm a single mother of five children, born and raised in Miami, Florida. I was born to two Haitian immigrants. My mom didn't speak English. However, my father spoke three languages. I grew up in a house with both parents and my five sisters and three brothers. My parents weren't married at the time, but already had three kids together before my time. My dad also had two daughters from a previous relationship before my mom. As my dad traveled back and forth to the states, he decided to make United States his home. He came to this country for better opportunities which would enable him to provide for his family in Haiti. He found a job as a carpenter at Regal Kitchens and began saving to get his own apartment.

Growing up, I always saw my father providing for my mother and his children and he never once spent the night out. My parents were working very hard and late at night. They would leave us with this old lady to take care of us while they worked. But I never understood why my parents were working so hard and not spending time with us until now. They came a long way. They even went back to get their other kids that they left in Haiti. This time both my parents had their legal residence green cards and applied for visas so that my siblings could come to the states. All of this was a process.

I was seven-years-old sitting on my daddy's lap while my mom was sitting on the couch. My brother and sister were sitting on the floor watching cartoons. I looked at my dad and said, "Daddy, if you love mommy so much, why don't you marry her?" He laughed and said, "Maybe I will." The next thing I knew my mom was planning this big wedding and I was the flower girl wearing these thick glasses with my hair in a ponytail. My sister and brother were the ring bearers. My mother was so beautiful in her long white dress. My aunt was her Maid of Honor. However, my dad was the coolest and most handsome guy I had ever seen. I was happy for them. To this day, my parents are still married with nine children, forty-seven grandchildren and eight great grandchildren. I always wanted to have what my parents had. They taught me love is about commitment and to put family first.

The preschool had eye exams one day and I was only five-years-old when I failed the test. They called my mom to inform her that I had my exam and they were referring me to an optometrist. My parents worked all of the time. But because my dad spoke and understood English, he took a day off to take me to Bascom Palmer Eye Institute. The doctor diagnosed me with high myopia, a degenerative disease where my glasses would have a high prescription and be thick. The doctor gave him the prescription and he took me to go get fitted for frames. The lady there said it would take longer than expected considering my prescription was so high. Three weeks later, my glasses were ready to be picked up. My dad picked my brother and I up from school and we headed to pick up my glasses. I didn't like them but I could see so clear. I've been wearing thick glasses since I was a little girl.

Growing up in elementary and middle school, you would think kids would pick on me, but I don't remember anybody calling me four eyes. I had plenty of friends and I was confident. Somehow, we were popular and some of the boys had a crush on me. But they were scared my brother and his friends would beat them up. I was the quiet one and my brother would always get in trouble. My brother dropped out of school in the seventh grade and he would ride his bike to meet us while me and my sister walked home from school.

I was in the 6th grade, but had a crush on an 8th grader. I was this skinny nerd and he never noticed me, although all of his friends did. I made straight A's and was always on the Honor roll. But now that we were in high school together, I thought maybe he would say hi, but he didn't. I think he had a girlfriend, but I didn't care. Before my freshman year of high school, my dad took me to my yearly eye exam at the eye institute. My doctor explained to my dad that they had contacts that would make my vision better. However, there were some risks if I didn't take care of them because I could get an infection. However, I wouldn't need those thick glasses anymore and I was so happy. They had to teach me how to wear them, but I learned easy. The contact lenses were expensive, but my parents sacrificed and paid for me to have them.

Life went on and I dropped out of school when I got pregnant at the age of 17. I was a senior dealing with a man 12 years older than me. I thought it was cool going to school while driving a box Chevy. My man taught me the street life because he was a drug dealer. My parents would threaten to call the police on him. After I gave birth to my daughter, they eventually accepted my baby daddy and allowed him to come to our house.

He had kids but I gave him his first and only girl. I named my baby after him. He was crazy about me but I wasn't crazy about him. One day, I was sitting on top of my baby daddy's car and he was standing next to me. The boy I was crazy about rode by on his bike and spoke to me. I gave him a look because my baby daddy was jealous and asked me if I knew him.

Months went by and I couldn't stop thinking about him. I called one of our mutual friends and told him how much I liked him. A few hours later, he called and asked me to come see him. I was excited to hear that he had been watching me. But I noticed he had baby mama drama because she called a hundred times. He told me she was crazy and that he liked me and wanted more. But I was still dealing with my baby daddy. I didn't want to leave the father of my child, but I was connected to this man. We kept in contact and talked on the phone for hours. Soon after, he went to jail and was charged with assault on a pregnant woman. He called me from jail and told me that his baby mama was pregnant with someone else's baby. He said she set him up and like a naive person, I believed him. He served a year in jail and I remained by his side. By that time, I had left my baby daddy and moved out of my parents' house. I was ready for him to come home. I furnished our home and purchased him a new wardrobe. I provided everything he needed because I fell in love with him.

I picked him up and we began our own family. I was on my third baby working as a security officer. One day I came home to a bunch of people in my house. I asked him why he wasn't answering his phone. He looked so mean and I knew he had been drinking. I was standing behind him while everybody was looking. Even his mother saw when he turned around and punched me in the eye. I was four months pregnant. I fell to the floor with my hands covering my face. He dragged me in the room and said, "Shut up bitch. Don't ask me shit."

His mom was calling his name as I was screaming, "Stop! I can't see!" He stopped and walked out of our room. His mom asked if I was okay. I was crying and scared because all I could see was black. I told her I needed to go to the hospital. He came back in the room and said, "Ain't shit wrong with her." He told me to take a shower and followed me into the bathroom. He was sitting on the toilet waiting with a towel in his hand. When I finished, he asked me why I embarrassed him. I didn't know what to say, so I told him I needed to see a doctor. I tried to lay down, but he wanted to have sex. I didn't want him to touch me. I told him I was hurt and couldn't see. He kissed my eye then pushed me on the bed. He tried to kiss me and I asked him to stop.

When he threatened to damage my other eye, I stopped pleading with him and asked what I did to deserve this. He told me to shut up in a soft tone and raped me. The next day, I begged him to take me to the hospital. My eye was still black and I couldn't see anything. He told me he was sorry and said he loved me. He told me not to tell anybody what really happened.

The doctor asked me what happened and I told him I tried to break up a fight and got hit. The doctor wanted to know why I would break up a fight since I was pregnant. He asked me if I wanted to talk to him alone, but my man was holding my hand too tight. I told the doctor we have no secrets.

The doctor said I had a retinal detachment and I had to have emergency surgery. I told him to call my parents, but he said "not yet". I had my surgery all alone. They couldn't put me to sleep because of the baby. I ended up having two surgeries, but both of them failed. It was too late. I was legally blind in my right eye. I stayed married to this man for 16 years. We had four boys together. I stayed because I wanted the family my parents had. But now I realize nothing changed. He was still abusive. I divorced him after all of those years. I finally did it, but my heart is still hurting.

Through Sickness and in Health
By: S.E. Newton

When I love you just doesn't seem like enough, that's when the ride starts to get rough. Explaining every yes, excusing every no, brushing off every insult not knowing I was adding to my existing injuries. I loved him harder than I ever loved any man before him, or so I thought. He was charming, caring, kind and his hands were soft to the touch. By the time he started to raise his hands, I was in too deep.

School was half-way over and clinicals were about to start. I was working and going to school full-time with a demanding schedule. Sixteen-hour days every Saturday and Sunday with an eight hour shift every Friday. The last thing I wanted to continue to deal with while I was preparing for our lives to change for the better were the insecurities of my soon to be husband. His life before me didn't change much after me, but I was no fool to the stresses and mismanagement of street life.

Crackheads or juugs, as we called them, were always unreliable on payday. The glory in knowing what his line of work was is that I knew it wasn't conducive to my lifestyle. But I hung my hope towards him based on one of the first conversations we had while we were getting to know one another. When I asked him about what he wanted to do for work since he never worked a day in his life, his response was "I like computers."

Often, I would question his level of competency when we would be out driving. He would read every sign as if he were either bored, getting used to reading out loud, or as if he was finding himself getting used to being with someone of my caliber. I mean, I never knew nor thought I was a threat or intimidating because of my education and thirst for knowledge. I brushed it off as boredom and accepted his "I like computers" response for what it was, short and basic.

I have never had an issue with being understanding, nor have I ever been in a rush to argue based on a blind assumption. Having his voice ring in my ear 'I like computers' led me to one day have a conversation with him when I got home from school. "What do you think about going to school to be a computer technician? You can get financial aid and go to school full-time while I work full-time as a scrub tech. You can even take courses online if you prefer." I was thinking about how most drug dealers enjoy their freedom to do whatever they want when they want. If he chose to take online courses, he would still have his freedom.

All I ever wanted to be was accommodating and to show him he could be loved unconditionally. His past wasn't my concern and his line of work was never appealing. The money he made from his most reliable clientele was lucrative, sure, but I knew his mama would always come first. Still, I didn't mind. His character and our vibe had me mesmerized. Until one day I grew tired of being sick and tired of the snide remarks and his emotional crippling behavior.

Our true end initiated the night he left to catch some money and didn't return within a reasonable time. I'm all for a man being a man when it comes to his personal time. Hell, even I need a break from time to time. But not making it home before the sunrise is an absolute no-no. I slept well that night, but I was not prepared for what I was about to discover.

It was 7 a.m. Sunrise came and went. He still wasn't at home or on his way through the door. I went back to sleep and called his mom when I woke up. Truthfully, I was hoping he went to her house knowing how I despised any man I was in a relationship with walking through my door past the crack of dawn. I got dressed and went downstairs to use the pay phone. Quarter after quarter, my hope for him being at her house was shaken by the sudden drop in my stomach.

She picked up, "Hello." Knowing I had to sound somewhat concerned and not anxious to be rid of her son, I said, "Good morning. I'm looking for your son. He didn't come home last night after making a run. It's not like him not to come home. Have you heard from him?" Her reply, I was not expecting. "He still down at BayFront, ain't he? Last I heard he was hit by a car and had to be rushed to the hospital." My arrogant selfishness for his well being escaped me, "Uh? What. Okay. I didn't know. I'm on my way now."

I didn't waste another minute getting to his side. If I could have run to the hospital without passing out, I would have. We lived a good twenty-minute walk from the hospital which was a quick five-minute drive if we had a car. I reinforced my medical training of remaining calm during a crisis with each stride I took. My immediate thought was, "I gotta get to him. He's been alone all this time." I panicked with grief from expecting the absolute worst every five minutes. As I was walking past the McDonald's, which was up the street from our apartment, tears began to stream down my face. I heard an unknown friendly voice yell out, "YOU NEED A RIDE!" Although I was in a state of emergency, I stayed true to us and refused the ride. He was the type of man who would not appreciate his woman looking at another man, let alone stopping to speak and respond to one.

His preference was well with my soul as I always kept to myself anyway, but in this instance concerning the offer of something so simple as a ride, all I could think was 'I don't know if he knows this man or someone he knows might be passing by'. The last thing we need is for an outsider to see me getting into another man's car, especially with him being in the hospital.' So many thoughts from an abused mind in such a little time, my reply as I never broke stride was, "Naw, I'm good. Thank you, though."

As I continued walking, I kept thinking who, what, and I'm pretty sure why, but I had to remain hopeful considering I wasn't abreast to his condition. The closer I got to the hospital emergency entrance, the more my heart dropped. Once I walked through the emergency room entrance and finally reached the intake specialist, I asked to see him. The wait to be taken back to where he was seemed like it was longer than my walk to the hospital. I took so many deep breaths the closer I got to his exam room. The nurse knew I needed to brace myself for what I was about to see. She whispered, "Stay calm".

I stepped closer to the bed and noticed he had the cover over his face as he usually does when he's asleep. I took a deeper breath and reminded myself just above a whisper to the nurse, "I know. I know." While I reached over his head to pull the sheet back, I called out his name as I unveiled the damage. The nurse felt the need to remind me again to stay calm. I respectfully quipped, "What are we waiting on? What's going on with him? What happened?"

She replied, "He was hit by a car and suffered cerebral hemorrhaging, a broken occipital and jawbone. He's going to need surgery. We're waiting for a room to open so we can relocate him upstairs. He's going to have to have surgery once the swelling goes down." I took another deep breath, shook my head, and blinked away a few more tears. I knew the road to his recovery was going to be a long one, but what I had not counted on were the increased mood swings and unbalanced behaviors now that he had suffered a traumatic brain injury (TBI).

When he finally got home after days of being in the hospital, a few things were discovered and a new temporary way of life laid in place. It was like we never skipped a beat. He didn't leave the house as much because he didn't like the damage the accident had done to his face. His face and skin were his most prized possessions. It was smooth, unblemished and dark chocolate.

His baby brother started visiting more frequently which eased my mind while I was at school and work. The damage that couldn't be measured is the fact that he also had anosmia. If he cooked anything and forgot a pot was on the stove, he wouldn't know it until he saw a fire since he could no longer smell.

I would have thought he would have smoked a little less weed because of this, but that was out of the question.

I hadn't counted on his need for me to chew the food he enjoyed the most since his jaw was wired shut for six weeks. I was relieved once he realized how uncomfortable chewing his food made me. Finally, I could use the food processor and he became okay with eating chicken noodle soup instead of hard ass wings from Gyros. I could never really tell just how much he was disturbed from the impact of his injuries, but I have to say they increased his insecure tendencies.

In spite of our relationship difficulties, I felt even more obligated to him and automatically took on his healing as though he was one of my rehab patients. Not the smartest, albeit one of the hardest things I have ever done or been to someone. I still wanted to leave him, but deep in my heart I held on to the hope of love, balance and understanding. Unfortunately, these things were on life support in our relationship. For the longest time, I questioned, "Would there ever be someone as understanding of his condition and ailments and not take advantage of him?" I no longer viewed him as my man, but just another person I had to take care of.

Through Sickness and in health
I told him I loved him and I meant it.
I showed him I loved him without restraint,
but he couldn't contain it.
I knew going into our marriage the
odds of us lasting were slim.
But I didn't want to believe I'd abused
love or love had abused me so
much so 'til my zeal for such a love would grow dim.

Through sickness and in health
One part of the vows that doesn't leave room for options,
But when physical abuse enters in, it brings with it room for
concussions.
What starts out as a simple joke of "I
was just playing" can later turn
into a Repeated life sentence of, "you know what I'm saying".

Through sickness and in health
The mind is where all seeds bud and
grow, turning one thought into
an action,
Which doesn't always lead to an opposite and equal reaction.
Choose to live and not die and don't worry, a love that's
'Through sickness and in health'
worthy will come in due time.

Additional Journal Prompts

How am I creating balance in my life?

What do I need to leave in my past?

What is my favorite positive affirmation and why?

What do I need to release today?

How am I better today than I was yesterday?

What is the 1 thing I need to say "No" to in my life right now?

What will I do to maintain my daily peace?

What do I need to declutter from my mind?

What am I grateful for?

What story am I telling myself?

What do I need to walk away from?

What did I smile about today?

What makes me smile?

What behaviors do I plan to release as I heal?

What gives me daily satisfaction?

What were my primary thoughts today and how did they influence my actions?

Transform 3 Negative thoughts into 3 Positive ones.

What am I Thinking, Feeling, and Imagining?

What will I prove to myself?

What vision do I have for my life?

What would I like to change about my life?

What is one thing I expected this week that I received?

What will my life be like when I step outside of my comfort zone?

What do I need to say YES to today?

When do I find it hardest to believe in myself?

How do I deal with the unexpected in a positive way?

What are the most important life values to me?

When was the last time I put myself first? How did that make me feel?

When I felt as though I could not go on, how did I find strength?

What can I do to begin thinking that my best is enough?

How do I embrace my imperfections?

What are some limiting beliefs I have about myself?

What am I inspired by?

What do I need to forgive myself for?

What do I value about myself?

How can I better respond to the challenges I'm currently facing?

How will I practice self-care today?

What habit do I need to break away from?

What is triggering me today?

What fresh beginning do I choose today?

Contributors

Harlo Hendrix refers to herself as a Middle-Aged Millennial and Renaissance Renegade. She is the former producer and re-occurring co-host on Saved N Sexy radio, an author, entrepreneur and community activist. She has written three publications under her pen name Toni Racell; one fictional novel called "Bread Pudding", a collection of stories and poems called "The Experience Chronicles", and her most recent semi-fictional series entitled, "Born Broken".

Harlo has a BFA in Visual Communications. She is also considered a light healer as a certified USUI RYOHO Reiki Master/Teacher and creates handmade healing jewelry. The proceeds go to her community efforts called "Candy Collective Project." Harlo is a wife, mother of 3 and grandmother of 3. She is a former Texas resident born in San Francisco, California, but considers Los Angeles her home. She currently resides in Las Vegas, NV.

Frederick Beaty was born and raised in Atlanta, GA. He has been actively writing since the age of 10. He is a Navy Veteran and served during Operation Desert Shield/Storm. He is a published author, active blogger, freelance writer, former radio show host, and social justice and political activist. Beaty strongly believes that Christians should be more active in the social justice, political, and human rights issues that plague us not only as a people, but as a nation.

Beaty's favorite saying is one he created: "It is impossible to enact forward progress when the path to understanding is impeded by those who do not wish to understand. This will always be the reason for conflict."

Janeice Smith-Alexandre is the wife of a Navy Veteran and a mother of two daughters. She received her Master's degree in Psychology with a concentration in School Counseling. She is currently a Certified School Counselor working in the Miami-Dade

County Public School System. She is also the CEO/ President of RIZE, Incorporated. RIZE's mission is to "restore healthy family dynamics by providing resources and encouragement that aids families in rising from their ashes."

Susie E. Newton is engulfed with her gift of helping and writing. Becoming a budding Project Manager, she has learned the balance of life and projects; the two things that used to overwhelm her. Having grown with the patience of Job, she never hesitates to tell others how she remains thankful to God for giving her the gifts he has entrusted to her. God has blessed her to own & successfully operate, God's Image Management & Consulting; a marketing, management & consulting company who's motto is "Where community meets business". G.I. Management & Consulting exists "to Break generational curses one stronghold at a time." These words have fueled her purpose actively since July of 2009.

With strategic marketing services offered through what was GI Music & GI Advertising is now RYB Network, an extension of Plays For A Purpose. This non-profit exists to promote unity within the community between sex, race, lifestyle, business and health. Her services cover a wide range of rebrand mentoring, talent and business development to ensure that your foundation is secure well past the statistically proven percentage of start-up businesses that fail within the first 5 years, just to name a few.

In efforts of rebranding Saved & Sexy Radio, she seasonally has both a full and developing staff of On-Air talent by whom all are Independent Authors, among other talents. Equipped with the knowledge of power and understanding, she began to move forward one layer at a time. Since the start of May 2014, Susie has steadily progressed and continued to remain focused through every possible distraction, one of which was her divorce in 2015, after five years. In the Fall of 2017, Susie reached the space and place where the release of what started out as a memoir turned inspirational Chronicles was released, one volume at a time starting with Constance Chronicles VOL III of V.

Mrs. Dorothy Pierre-Joseph is the owner and operator of Heartbrake to Breakthrough, LLC. She is an alumni of North Miami Senior High School. She received her BS in Biology at Barry University and completed her Nursing degree at Indian River State College. Mrs. Pierre-Joseph is currently conducting a multi-city Trauma Tour titled the "Flipside" that promotes healing and deliverance from past and current trauma and teaching in the areas of breaking attachments, identifying triggers, breaking trauma cycles and more. For over 9 years, she has worked as a Registered Nurse with over 7 years of experience as a psychiatric nurse advocating for mental health and wholeness. Dorothy is an ordained minister who has been featured in the Bridge Magazine and as a speaker at numerous engagements and conferences. Most recently, she was esteemed as an honorary speaker at The Long Hallway Movie Premiere to raise awareness concerning domestic violence. You can catch her teaching, encouraging, and inspiring through her syndicated podcast show "The Breakthrough" on iTunes and Anchor Radio. She is a mother of 5, wife to a wonderful husband and active participant at her house of worship at All Nations Life Development Christian center and in her community. As a multi-trauma survivor, she accredits her healing, accomplishments, and life's purpose to the almighty God. "Wherefore the rather, brethren, give diligence to make your calling and election sure: for if ye do these things, ye shall never fall (2 Peter 1:10)."

Tahira Walker was raised in Bridgeton, New Jersey. She attended Bridgeton High School and graduated in 2011. She's also in the U.S. Air Force Air National Guard. She completed her basic training in May 2017. Walker has a mentoring organization called "Blooming Roses" for girls aged 6-10. Walker's main focus is to help the community, help the youth, and be the best mother to her daughter. Lastly, Walker plans to open a youth center in her community for kids to have something positive to do instead of turning to guns, violence, and negative activities.

Tarena Tutt is an entrepreneur, activist, writer, cancer fighter, and mother of four wonderful children. She strives to inspire and help others in the world from different walks of life. She volunteers often in the community working with at-risk teens and adults. Her goal in life is to continue helping others directly or indirectly connect to the next positive level of their lives.

About the Author

Latrice Scott was born and raised in Miami, Florida and is a Licensed Mental Health Counselor. Scott has over 10 years of experience in the Mental Health field. As a platform to continue creating quality projects, NaScot Publishing, LLC was established in 2015. NaScot Publishing, LLC's mission is to help individuals express themselves through writing. With this intent in mind, the motto, "Revealing the Story in You" was birthed. Mental Remote Network, LLC was established in 2017 to provide counseling services to under-served populations. MRN's motto is 'Meeting You Where You Are'. Scott's first published book is entitled "Hit or Miss". She has since published "Evolution of Human Emotions" and "Hit or Miss 2". Scott's sole focus is to help aspiring authors to reveal the stories within them and teach others how to heal Mind, Body, & Spirit.

FB: Nascot Publishing, LLC
    Healing Hurt Hearts Private Facebook Community

IG: @nascotpublishing_
    @mytraumajournal
    @mentalremotenetwork
    Website: www.mytraumajournal.com

For speaking engagements, contact me at: 1-877-828-4148

Resources

National Suicide Prevention Lifeline- 1-800-273-8255 or "988"

National Domestic Violence Hotline- 1-800-799-7233

~Chat- Text "START" to 88788

National Sexual Assault Hotline- 1-800-656-4673

SAMHSA National Helpline- 1-800-662-4357

Disaster Distress Helpline- 1-800-985-5990

National Problem Gambling Helpline- 1-800-522-4700

Mental Remote Network, LLC- 1-877-828-4148 (Non-crisis)

www.griefshare.org

www.mhanational.org/find-support-groups

Notes

<barcode>||| | | ||| | || ||| || |||| ||| || |||| |||| ||| ||| | | || |||</barcode>

<barcode>||| | | ||| | || ||| || |||| ||| || |||| |||| ||| ||| | | || |||</barcode>

Printed in the United States
by Baker & Taylor Publisher Services